Peregrine

2020   **Volume XXXIV**

Managing Editors	Ellen Summers
	Janet Summers
Poetry Editors	Rachelle M. Parker
	Ellen Summers
Prose Editor	Janet Summers
Layout	Janet Summers
Publisher	Amherst Writers & Artists Press
Editor, AWA Press	Jan Haag

Amherst Writers & Artists Press, Inc.
P.O. Box 1076
Amherst, MA 01004
Phone: 413 253 3307

peregrine@amherstwriters.org
www.amherstwriters.org

Peregrine is published annually. Submission details are available at amherstwriters.org or peregrinejournal.submittable.com. Payment is in copies. The editors endorse the practice of simultaneous submissions.

Copies are available on amazon.com for $12.

Amherst Writers & Artists (AWA) affiliates offer writing workshops for adults, youth, and children across the world. In addition, AWA sponsors public readings and maintains an international training program that supports the work of writers and artists. Amherst Writers & Artists Press, Inc., publishes *Peregrine*, books of poetry and fiction, and the Amherst Writers & Artists poetry chapbook series.

Cover art by Barry Moser (used with permission)
Peregrine nesting sketch by Karen Buchinsky (used with permission)

CONTENTS

Peregrine Tribute to Pat Schneider

Patricia Vought Schneider, June 1, 1934–August 10, 2020

Peregrine began as a "dream of a journal," in Pat Schneider's words, at the same time Amherst Writers & Artists was coming into existence in the early 1980s. Two original AWA board members, Elizabeth Finn French and Walter Rumble, wanted to launch a literary journal. They got to work, along with Pat and other board members, and, when the first issue was ready to go to press in 1983, they needed a name for it.

Pat loved to tell the story about how Elizabeth Finn French suggested *Peregrine.* "Our first reaction was, 'huh?'" Pat wrote. "Elizabeth told us that not only was the peregrine falcon an endangered species, and not only had a sheltered nest and a mated pair been placed on top of UMass's new library building, but also the word meant 'pilgrim' (from the Latin *perigrinus*). We accepted the title."

The first issue consisted of thirty-five stapled pages that sold for $3. To the end of her days, one of the things Pat was most proud of about AWA was that it publishes an annual literary journal that solicits and accepts poetry and prose from writers all over the world. Pat's death coincided with the publication of the thirty-fourth issue of *Peregrine*, the one you hold in your hands.

To say that we miss her does not begin to express our grief and our love for the woman who created the supportive AWA method that represents everything Pat Schneider believed about writing. That a writer is someone who writes. That everyone has a strong, unique voice, and everyone is born with creative genius. And perhaps most important, that writing as an art form belongs to all people, regardless of economic class or educational level.

Not only did she codify the method and detail it in her book, *Writing Alone and With Others* (Oxford University Press, 2003), Pat shared it with the world, training others to lead writing workshops that have spread across the globe. Every day AWA workshop leaders help writers gain confidence in their voices and devote themselves to making literary art.

Peregrine is only one of Pat Schneider's many gifts to the writers who have been published in it, and to its readers, for more than three decades. We are proud to carry on her legacy in these annual slim volumes that hold the work of so many talented writers.

And though it's hard to think of AWA without Pat, we know that *Peregrine* will continue to thrive like those namesake birds that have flourished at UMass and around the Amherst region. We trust that Pat's spirit flies, too, landing now and again to remind us that we are pilgrims forever in search of words, and that our words are worthy of the page.

Jan Haag, AWA Press editor
Ellen Summers, Peregrine *co-managing editor*
Janet Summers, Peregrine *co-managing editor*
Rachelle M. Parker, Peregrine *poetry editor*
Karen Buchinsky, Peregrine *emerging writers editor*
The AWA Board of Directors

Celebrating Bisi Ideraabdullah

Bisi Ideraabdulah is a powerhouse. She's the kind of person you want on your team—and she's all about team. As hard as she works, from morning to exhaustion, she's the first to tell you she can't do it all; she'll get you to help, too. She says she's a "we" person. Bisi is a hard-working, humble woman, warm and easy to talk to. When you speak to her, you know you are being listened to—you're being heard. She is helping to heal our broken world here in the U.S. in Brooklyn, New York, and in Liberia, Africa.

Years ago, in labor, Bisi was denied entry to a racist hospital in South Carolina, and her baby girl, Imani, died as a result. Imani means "faith." Bisi had other children; she could not give up. She, her husband, and their five other children emigrated to Liberia and founded Imani House, initially aiding in relief efforts for women and ex-combatants, and teaching people sustainable farming. Now, Liberia's Imani House has a full-service maternal and child healthcare clinic, plus adult literacy programs serving over 1,800 people a year. Recently, Imani House has begun working with the Liberian Marketing Association, introducing a program to bring literacy classes to market women. In addition, the organization has started a peer-education program, training teens on sexual health, pregnancy and STD prevention, as well as teaching them to facilitate workshops on the topic in various schools.

On a trip back to the U.S. to find additional support, Bisi realized that her hometown, Brooklyn, had many people who needed assistance as well. The organization's first U.S. project started in 1994, a program to help those with low literacy levels, mainly immigrants. Since then Imani House programs have met the diverse and growing needs of Brooklyn and Liberian communities. In the U.S., it directly serves over 1,200 low-income families, youth, immigrants, and elderly each year. Through community outreach, workshops, and forums, it indirectly serves an additional 4,000.

Since her return to the U.S., Bisi has given generously of herself to Amherst Writers & Artists. She has supported AWA with her energy and insight through times of crisis, serving on the board of directors for many, many years, and taking on special projects as needed. She has been part of a team of trainers of the AWA workshop-leader method, and leads her own writing workshop, Women of Color. Bisi is truly one of the mothers of AWA.

In spite of her overloaded schedule, when I need to talk, she finds some time. I suspect I am not the only person for whom this is true. She is a lovely, inspirational person, sorely needed in this world, and I am honored to speak for the AWA board, staff, and hundreds of affiliates in dedicating this issue of *Peregrine* to her.

Thank you, Bisi, for everything.

Autobiography

Bisi Ideraabdullah is a Brooklyn-born educator, activist, humanitarian, wife, and mother of five children. In 1998 she became the first recipient of AWA's Elizabeth G. Berryhill Scholarship, and took AWA workshop training under Pat Schneider. She credits her twenty-one-year-old workshop and her writing through the traumas of war to her friend, mentor, and activist, Pat Schneider.

Her story is one of courage and determination. In 1982, her life changed when she went into critical labor while on vacation in South Carolina. The first hospital she and her husband reached treated them as if they weren't there and turned them away. This resulted in the death of their daughter, Imani. The Ideraabdullahs were private business owners in Miami, Fla., but Bisi was depressed, disillusioned, and tired of acts of bias and discrimination. In 1985, less than three years later, she moved her family to Liberia, West Africa.

In 1986, she and her husband founded Imani House Liberia and set up educational programs in honor of their daughter. When, five years later, in 1990, Liberia's civil war erupted, the family made a decision to stay in Liberia and help. In spite of the dangers and bombings in her area, she began volunteering and was made a ward director at a local clinic.

In 1991, when thousands of refugees fled into an open field adjacent to her family's land, she worked with UNFCU, UNICEF, and others to install wells, distribute supplies, and set up urban agricultural and literacy programs. She secured a tent from the U.N. and set it up to treat and care for the displaced. She and her husband also created a home and school for thirty abandoned children along with training and literacy programs for victims of the war.

Determined to help end the war, Bisi used much of her family's money for this work. She returned to the U.S. several times to raise awareness and funds, and to participate in anti-war activities. In the U.S. she collected urgently needed supplies and shipped containers. In 1993, she built the Imani House Maternal and Child Healthcare Clinic in Liberia. The clinic has never shut its doors through thirteen years of war, staff kidnappings, Ebola, financial crisis, and now COVID-19. It treats upwards of 18,000 Liberians each year. It is a beacon in the community it serves.

In late 1996, after almost seven years of brutal war, she and her children finally returned to the U.S. while her husband remained in Liberia working for the U.N. Unable to sit idle, she managed her

Liberia projects remotely and founded Imani House New York in a small storefront in Park Slope. Without money or paid staff, she recruited volunteers and started a free food pantry, adult literacy/ESOL classes for immigrants, and children's computer classes. Today in addition to the clinic and literacy programs in Liberia, Imani House New York works from three locations providing after-school and summer camps for hundreds of children and adult education for immigrant students.

After her AWA training in 1998, Bisi Ideraabdullah founded WOC (Women of Color Writers Workshop). WOC's first publication in 2002 was *Voices of Brooklyn: Writings from the Women of Color Writers Workshop*. WOC is completing *Boundaries & Borders*, a collection of writing from women of color across the globe. Her story "Imani Means Faith" appears in the National Book Foundation's Collection, *Sounds of This House*. Bisi's memoir, *How Many Days Until Tomorrow*, is expected out soon.

In spite of everything, Bisi never wavered on her children's needs. She and her husband are proud parents of successful adults: a genetic scientist, a pediatrician, an aerospace engineer, and a retired Coast Guard officer, and her oldest son works in human services in New York.

For more information, visit www.imanihouse.org or WOCWriters@imanihouse.org.

Dedicated to my mentor, friend, and sister, Pat Schneider

In Search of Liberty—An Illusion

Liberia, West Africa, April 6–11, 1996—Civil War

On April 6, 1996, Liberia's civil war was over six years old. But it was far from over. Instead, the hope that the thirteenth ceasefire agreement would hold was gone. War had broken out again, and the carnage that began on that day would escalate into one of the worst attacks on the capital city of Monrovia since the war started six years earlier.

Just after dawn on Saturday, April 6, desperate calls began filtering into my bedroom through my husband's two-way radio. U.N. personnel, mostly insulated and protected during the war, were frantic. A woman's anxious voice said, "I see a man through my window. He's lying beside a car. They shot him!" Another said, "What's happening? What's going on? Oh God, they are right outside my window!" Their questions and statements tumbled out and over each other, some in whispers, all pleading.

Mahmoud grabbed his radio and bolted upright, seated on the edge of the bed; he was rubbing his eyes and feeling around in the sheets for his eyeglasses.

The children were still asleep. I whispered, "What's going on, Mahmoud? What's happening now?" He slumped his shoulders and shook his head. Once I understood what people were saying and heard the machine guns popping in the background, I knew exactly what was going on. I raised my voice in disgust, "Jesus, how can this be happening again?"

At the end of 1989, Charles Taylor began Liberia's civil war. His stated objective was to oust President Samuel K. Doe—the first indigenous president of Liberia. But even though Doe had been tortured and killed by September 1990, the war continued. Several ethnically allied rebel groups formed across the country, rampaging, killing hundreds of thousands of people, and looting and pillaging the country's gold and diamond resources.

Mahmoud stared at the small radio-phone as call after call vibrated through it and merged with the sounds of machine guns. The U.N. heads of security broke in several times to ask people what was going on or to calm them. No one seemed to know what was happening or who was fighting whom. But that was how this insane war was. There were so many warring factions that it was never clear who was fighting.

The calls kept coming. A woman's terrified voice said, "What should I do? Can someone please come for me? She cried, "What should I do…?

Mahmoud spoke to them with his usual calm, "Please stay in your homes." He added, "If they come inside your house, give them what they want. They won't hurt you. Just give them what they want." I didn't believe that, and neither did he. The soldiers were usually drunk and unpredictable.

Turning to me, he looked confused. What could he do, what should he do? His office was about seven miles away. He had a low-level U.N. position that didn't provide him a vehicle. And our pickup was not reliable. But he was looking at me for an answer. All I could say was, "Do you wanna go?" I was hoping he'd say no. No, that he would not leave his family to manage U.N. radio communications. But he said nothing.

I knew they needed him, plus he really wanted to go. I turned to face him, "They need you, don't they?" He shook his head, yes. I looked at him for a pause, shrugged my shoulders, and said, "Then you should go." He half smiled, started getting dressed, and told U.N. security that he was on his way to the office. Relieved, they thanked him more than once, then continued to try to assuage those calling while ordering staff into the field to find out what was happening.

Before he left, Mahmoud pecked me on the cheek and promised me he'd be back after work. I told him, "Be careful. We'll be OK. See you later." But I felt let down that he did not choose us over the U.N. This was a problem that often led to disagreements between us. He did not return that night, or the next, or the next.

We were able to speak for the first couple of days through our two-way radios. On day three, he told me he was OK but wanted clean clothes. Mahmoud will always tell you he is OK. He said that he and his staff were the only ones in the building, that they had slept on the floor. As I dug deeper, asking if he'd seen any rebels and when he was coming home, he told me that there was no way to cross the bridges to get home. That there was heavy fighting on them, and no one could pass. It surprised me when he added in the same "it's OK" tone, "But I think they are almost in the building,"

"Who?" I said. "Who is almost in the building?"

"Rebels," he said. "They're outside. I hear the glass on the vans breaking."

"What!" I yelled. "Can you get out of there?"

He hesitated, then said, "I don't think we will be in here much longer. They're already on the stairs." I kept talking, but he didn't respond. "Mahmoud, is there a back way out?"

That was it, his radio was silent, but I kept calling him using his U.N. call sign. "Delta eight. Delta eight. Come in, delta eight. Can you read me, delta eight?" There was nothing. My eyes filled up and ran over; I was so scared. I had no idea what might have happened to him once the rebels went in, and there was no way for me to find out. I would find out later that the rebels entered, took everything from them, and marched him and his staff out of the building at gunpoint.

By the end of the first day, I'd learned that this new invasion was started by Charles Taylor and his ragtag army of boy soldiers. He came into the city to attack one of his adversaries, Roosevelt Johnson. Taylor's boys were among the worst. They were vicious and unapologetic, and they didn't care who you were. They waged more war against civilians than soldiers, mostly because they could steal from civilians. Most were drugged young kids with big guns and not much conscience. These boys were no longer boys, even though many were ten to fifteen years old. They were unpredictable and dangerous. But it didn't make sense that the U.N. West African peacekeepers who usually came between the warring factions when they fought in the capital could not or would not stop them this time.

The fighting and looting continued. And while rocket-propelled grenades, bombs, and heavy machine-gun fire reverberated through the house, I wondered just how much more of this we could take. The smells of burning and death had long replaced the safety and tranquility that I'd hoped to find when we moved to Liberia eleven years ago.

By April 10, day four, we no longer ventured out. My daughter's friend, Ade, came to hide in our home because the rebels were after a BBC reporter who was close to his sister. People in the neighborhood warned Ade's sister that men with guns were looking for her. Apparently, the BBC reporter angered the rebels when he divulged Taylor's excessive and indefensible murders of civilians. Ade was afraid they might kill him to get to his sister. This boy was like my son. He'd been friends with my children and our family for years. I had to let him stay with us. He told me his sister would get him out of Liberia the next day—and she did.

So we were confined to the house, Mahmoud was missing, and still, I refused even to consider leaving Liberia. I really did believe that the fighting would stop again, and the war would end this time.

But each night, when the sun would start to go down and sounds of war went up, we'd try to secure the house. The girls and I would lift the rusted, five-foot metal pole into its slots across the front door frame while the boys helped push the old gas stove out of the kitchen, over the tile floor, and against the door. We then lifted at least two bags of rice, each one weighing a hundred pounds, and added some large bags of flour and sugar on top of that. We'd light the kerosene lanterns and close the curtains. Barricading the door brought a sense of security, but not much, because we'd already had one home invasion, and outside, sometimes close by and sometimes in the distance, the sounds of chaos and murder raged.

Afterward, we'd settle down in the living room, away from all the windows. Sometimes I'd see my children looking at me. But I rarely let them see how worried I was. At least I think they didn't notice. That night while they gathered around their friend laughing and telling stories as if there was no war, no one dying, and no one coming to break the door down, I was frazzled. The fighting and home invasions were getting worse. My stomach was in knots, and the palms of my hands alternated between being blood red and freezing. Seeing the children playful and unconcerned helped me many times to make excuses for why we were still in Liberia.

As they chatted and gossiped with their friend, I remember looking up at the oversized painting that hung over our hefty collection of books about African civilizations and history. I loved this piece of art and brought the original with us from the States. Modeled after the series "Roots," it shows two strong black hands holding a child toward the sky—toward God. It was an accurate portrayal of hope, our hopes for happiness and safety for ourselves and our children when we moved to Liberia in 1985. But those hopes were vanishing. I was tired, worn out, and beginning to lose all confidence that the war would ever satisfy the appetites of the greedy, murderous warlords or come to an end.

By Sunday, April 11, the entire city was burning. I didn't know the whereabouts of my husband, I was afraid for my children, especially my girls, and I was exhausted.

On the morning of Monday, April 12, 1996, six days after the invasion, my children and I were airlifted by helicopter out of Liberia. As we waited in an open field protected by the peacekeeping forces, I learned of a Lebanese man who had a two-way radio. I approached his car, and he smiled and asked how he could help me. I told him that I didn't know where my husband was and that I'd lost communications with him when rebels drove him out of the U.N.

building on Mamba Point. He asked me his name. When I told him, Mahmoud, he said he knew him and that he had seen him at the U.S. Embassy helping people get registered to leave.

The man tuned the radio, made a call, and said, "Abdullah, I have someone here who would like to speak to you." He then handed the radio to me, and after I excitedly said hello, Mahmoud replied, "Hello, Bisi," as if he'd just seen me that morning. I called all of the children over to speak to him. We couldn't stay on the radio too long, but Mahmoud said he was OK, just dirty with no change of clothes and that he would meet us wherever they took us once he could leave.

We slept overnight in that field to sounds of the war raging just outside of its gates. The children slept on the ground, and I slept with my youngest son and daughter in the back seat of a friend's pickup. We were reunited with Mahmoud a little over one week after we arrived in Senegal. Although the embassy rented a hotel to house the people they airlifted and made loans to fly us back to the States, I refused. Instead, we rented an apartment in Dakar and stayed in Senegal for the next four months.

I hoped that once the fighting in Liberia stopped, we'd be able to return home. It was devastating to even consider returning my family to the U.S. where we, as Black people, would be forced to go back to a position of second-class citizenship. I felt that a return to the States, in the midst of everything else we had to face, was the worst thing that could happen to us.

Sojourn

Camino

Somewhere we will leave a stone on a mound of rocks,
walk and walk to the end and the sea, where we'll throw
our last shell back into salt-brine.

The rhythm of footfall, femur, pelvis
and swaying sacrum will soothe and soften
the knots deep in our thoughts,

bodies and bones. We hope this journey
will bring us back to being
the bipedal creatures we are, nomads

on this land—hunters of beauty,
gatherers of stories, who seek still
to love. Even as we domesticate and cultivate,

we are wanderers, our steps as numerous
as the stars. We were made
to walk softly on this earth, to leave a trace

imprint in sand soon impressed
under other soles treading the same sacred places.

What Good Husbands Do

Thirty minutes before pictures, my wife is hunting for Mia's pink dress. She ransacks the bedroom and living room, pulling everything from both closets. I'm on the couch finishing a book, sipping soda through a curly straw.

She stops in front of me, sweating. She hasn't sweated since the delivery. "By the way, I didn't need four bladed razors," she says. "The cheap ones work fine."

She yanks out a box of Mia's stuff wedged under the coffee table and dumps it over the couch. Just a bunch of shirts and swaddles, no pink dresses. "Well, at least check on Mia," she says. "You don't want her rolling over, do you?"

My book goes across the table. I head to the bedroom. As expected, Mia's sleeping fine, so I march into the bathroom and dump the top drawer. Expensive hair care products everywhere. I launch each one into the trash can. For the $50 conditioner she bought, I lean back and nail a three-point shot.

Then my wife barrels in, demanding I stop acting like a child. On the sink next to her are the four bladed razors, still in the pack, still untouched.

I dig my nice jeans and tee shirt out of the hamper. But I'm not messing with my hair. It's good enough. My wife swings in, shaking her head. "These pictures are expensive," she says. She faces the mirror and puts on her lipstick. "Those jeans are wrinkled like hell," she says. Then she boosts Mia from the crib and takes her to the car.

At the first light, I tell my wife that I understand her stress. "I get why you haven't been yourself," I say. "You've got too much on your plate." Then I press the gas and speed through the light. "So, from now on, I'll do the laundry and you won't have to worry about forgetting it."

The lady taking the pictures is all smiles, all excitement about her kids. Apparently, her youngest graduated pre-school with honors and her oldest married a girl from the rotary club. During the break, she squeezes next to my wife on the couch, hikes up a pants leg, and points at the top of her sock.

"Aren't these the cutest?" the lady says. "You know, I only asked Bob for cheap socks. But he thought the pigs looked cute." I look at my wife, then the lady. I finally open my mouth: "Bob is a great guy. He bought the better socks because he loves you."

My wife holds my arm the whole way home, then takes Mia to the crib and makes dinner. It's the first home-cooked meal in a long time. After loading the dishwasher, she says she wants to tell me something.

"It's already past nine," I say.

She takes my arm and escorts me into the bedroom where she takes off her clothes and slides under the covers. "Okay, so what is it?" I ask.

"I just wanted to tell you that I love that lady's socks."

Hades Sets the Record Straight

It was never about love to me. That makes a better story, but
I did not love her when I split the ground and dragged her down
to my world. I did not love her when I slipped seeds into her
wine to be swallowed. I needed a woman who could nurture

and grow small sprouts among the asphodels, flood the fields
with everlasting flowers golden in the thick grass. I wanted
a woman who would not wilt completely under the weight
of earth and its demands, rocks heavier than any crown.

I am heartless. Everyone agrees on this. Sitting in judgement,
exiled to a realm no one else wanted: surrounded by shades,
gleaming with gems, rich and remote. Oldest son and least
loved. Passive, impartial as death. Impossible to care for

my charges when I am only a quiet scythe, waiting and cold.
Only a living thing can. Only a woman knows how to tend.

Holiday

We stay home and put up the tree.
White, with funfetti colored lights,
all burnt out from last year.

Of course, I order more to spare my children
another disappointment. I forgot to buy the turkey—
my only job—and when it came time for dinner,
we didn't go.

I couldn't be at my sister's house—everyone
drinking, smiling, reminiscing on the year.
The last time I held a baby, it was my own
dead baby. Doll-like, cold.

Solvable games, puzzles, a glass of wine—
I am the one with the weight of the dying
on her chest. Like a good ghost,
I can watch but cannot change anything.

This Life

In this life
We may never get it right

We dance
And flutter
with your skin
Just out of my reach

The music in another room
The scent of chocolate from
A bakery not yet open
The sun casting
A rainbow through the window

In this life
I may never hold you in my arms
again
But that doesn't mean
I will ever stop
Checking my watch
To see if the bakery doors
Are about to open

ESSAM M. AL-JASSIM,

TRANSLATOR, ARABIC ORIGINAL BY HAMDAN ATIA*

The Leap of Joy

Fourteen women shepherded and cared for goats in the heart of Africa. Some carried young children on their backs while others sang sad songs about their missing men. The backdrop of the sunset further accentuated the sullen and sorrowful outlook that captured the dire essence of the world.

The horizon revealed nothing more than an exhausted, emaciated black face that served as a guide for the white pirates who sought a bottle of beer or a pack of cigarettes. When the pirates saw the women, they charged at them. They violently snatched the babies from their shoulders, whirling them around, slashing and hacking at their bodies as if they were rodents. They girded the women and tied them up like cattle. The whip marks shone on their scraggy, skinny backs and raised swollen red streaks. The pirates followed these welts with the ship-owner's name—a brand to facilitate buying and selling. They cast upon the unfortunate women indelible scars, which would remain forever—as a horrific reminder of their tragic past.

The women shambled as they walked across the sweltering heat of the desert. The only sounds were the crunching of sand and the moaning and sighing of crippled women thinking of their helpless children who had been left badly disfigured and mutilated, if not dead. But it was useless; they were easy prey for lions by now.

When they finally reached the shore, a cargo ship was waiting for them. The pirates led the women to the deck, chained them together by their necks with shackles and read out instructions for the voyage. "Talking and singing are forbidden. You are to remain silent for the duration of the journey. Those defying orders will face brutal beatings till death. We'll fetter and pack every group close to each other to optimize the available space."

As soon as the fourteen women were chained together, resilience swept through their weary eyes. After a lifetime of hardship, their moment of escape had arrived. Their leap was one of relief and joy: a feast for the ocean.

*Atia, Hamdan, *A Trader of Clouds* (Cairo: General Egyptian Book Organization, 2016).

Breakfast

I want the honest
smell of citrus. I want

each downstairs
curtain drawn, filtered
sun filling the room.

Car shadows speed across
the wall like hunched,
hurried bodies.

Out there,
crows fruit the trees—
heavy and shining.

Day lilies, storm-
splayed, lie
ragged and shamed.

Spruces bend to wind until
they cannot unbend.

With all its demands
the body is an unyielding negotiator.

Cupping water to my lips,
I race the greedy gaps
between my fingers.

Mother's Day

Harold Kapoor eyed the purple flowers that are his daughter's namesake and frowned. He got irises last year, but they were his wife's favorite, hence their daughter's name. She loved the deep purple color and the way they fanned out from the center. He clutched red roses in his hand tighter, the flowers from their wedding. Myra would've had their whole wedding purple, if she'd gotten her way. Too bad her mother knew the wedding planner.

"Can I help you, sir?" Harold turned around. A young woman with a blonde bob and a wide smile stood behind him in the flower shop's uniform: a white button up shirt and khaki pants. He must have looked confused. He'd found that since he entered his 80s, he'd been looking that way more and more, even to himself in the mirror. The wire-rimmed glasses he'd purchased last year and scars that speckled his thinly skinned face didn't help.

"I'm trying to decide what flowers to get my wife," he said.

The woman nodded. "Mother's Day? What are your options?"

He held the roses out. "These, or the irises."

She scrunched up her nose and put a hand to her face. "I personally like the roses. But we get you a bouquet with both."

Harold shook his head. "No, just the roses, then."

"Alrighty." She led him to the register, and he paid for the roses. He looked around the shop, where he'd gotten Myra flowers every year for the last 50 years or so. The shop had painted the walls twice over the years, from pale yellow to white to sky blue. They'd never changed the red door, though, or the cream tiled floor.

"Your wife is very lucky," the young woman said, handing Harold his change. "My boyfriend can barely remember my birthday."

Harold offered her a crooked smile and left with his flowers.

He took the long way back. He passed the duck pond on his way, where he and Myra used to feed the ducks. They went once when Myra was pregnant with Iris. Belly round and pulsing with their daughter's possibilities, Myra ate more bread than she threw. She laughed when Harold pointed this out for her. "I'm eating for our baby girl," she said, and stuffed another chunk of bread in her mouth. Harold watched his wife toss crumbs at the ducks and felt his heart fill with her.

Harold passed the diner where he and Myra went on their first date and the local elementary school, where kids were just getting out for the day, flocking to their parents with bright eyes and book bags full of math sheets and pencil stubs. He passed the bar he used to go to after work and the office building where he used to spend his days as an accountant, pictures of his wife and baby girl on his desk.

It took him thirty minutes to reach the hill where he'd meet Myra, whereas it would have taken a younger Harold fifteen, but he didn't mind the walk. He took the bouquet in both hands and made his way through the local cemetery, weaving through the graves of the recently passed. He found Myra somewhere in the middle, her grave clean even though the date of death had been written 45 years prior. Next to her, their baby girl in a miniature coffin. He hadn't wanted to see either of them after the accident, to keep them whole in his memory, but he'd done it. Had he not owed it to them, as the sole survivor?

He laid the roses on Myra's grave, and took a single stem from the dozen. He placed it gently over Iris' name. Placing a kiss on his fingertips, he touched the gravestones and stood. He preferred to spend the rest of the holiday remembering how it used to be. He'd bring the flowers home to Myra, roses or irises or once even white lilies, for a change. They'd go out to their favorite diner with Iris in tow, feeling invincible in the love for them both.

You Just Wanted to Sleep

Cabbage, radar, iron,
images in a cave,
now in your childhood
home where you are taking
inventory of where furniture
stood on casters, in the 1970s
and then in the last year. The
shag carpet, strewn with
invisible flowers, the drapery
that matched the sofa that
matched the yellow dishes,
that matched the winter sheets,
that matched the bedroom
slippers and lamp cover,
under which father ate
salted boiled peanuts, loading
them into Brew 102 as he drank it
down nightly before
the throat of dinner
was served on the round table.
Garlic, iron, shark, a book you read
In Hawaii the summer the family
booked a tour of the black
sand beach and you wanted to be
afraid of Salem's Lot,
the photo of a girl with blood
on her mouth. And the wild seawater,
deceptively calm, that sucked
you under when you tried to stray
from the steady coast of your life.

Mr. Dente

My seven-year-old, Lydia, took my hand, and said with a shark's grin, "Daddy thinks Mr. Dente is cute too, don't you Daddy?"

Mr. Dente, her math teacher, six feet tall and a mass of ebony muscle, paused, and then softly smiled at Lydia. I imagined him curling his dark fingers around my caramel neck, my solitary chance to know the gospel of his beauty.

I wasn't out. I have known I was queer since four. I gave heterosexuality the good ole college try for my parents, thus my little angel. My parents feigned surprise when I divorced. I would have avoided Mr. Dente, but every week he counseled me about Lydia's deluge of bad grades. He could like men, too, I thought, but who would bet on that with this leviathan of a man? Why risk it? Mr. Dente might kick me to death and beat a murder rap claiming he panicked, despite how peacocks like him preen themselves.

"Lydia, this is about your grades," I said.

Lydia pouted.

"Are we clear?"

"Yes, sir."

Mr. Dente cleared his throat. "Mr. Trent, Lydia will need summer school. I feel this would be best for your daughter's advancement."

Mr. Dente reached in his desk and pulled out a pamphlet. He took a business card from his Rolodex, reached for a pen, hesitated, then wrote on it and passed them both to me. I tried to shake his hand, but his obsidian mitt engulfed my little pumpkin paw.

I looked at the business card with his full name, Alonso Dente, the number for the school's front office, his class phone, and his school e-mail. When I flipped it over, I saw, "Let's get a drink sometime ;)," a cell phone number, and an address. I mused on Lydia's insight before slipping his card into my pocket.

Dimly Shining Moon

A fingernail moon hangs in the night sky
a solitary brightness
among the urban light-drowned darkness
shining bravely on, little beacon to us.

My son would point it out,
as a toddler,
would marvel at it
though I don't know what he thought of it.
Who knows what ideas form in minds that young?
Now he is 14, of course he's
much too cool to look up at the moon.

Though not as cool as his friends,
who tease him about marching band,
who didn't get into his geometry class
and shamed him out of letting us drive him to school.

I know how he feels:
a beacon of brightness
among a middle school of dimmed bulbs
hardly daring to shine.

How Them Became Us

How we bowed. How they smoked an entire mosque, so we would choose a different God. How they shut the TV when Hannah Montana had her first kiss, so we would forget how to love. How they learned how to make falafel and called it vegan cakes. How they made us take our hijabs off, only to see us put them back on in the markets. How they tried to forgive themselves. How they needed to be right. How they slept. How they didn't. How they learned Arabic to heal their tongues, only to wake up one morning to find their throats choking on our letters. How they made us teach them how to swallow, not knowing they would have to taste the char of our olive trees, and then our grandparents. *How,* they needed to know. Hand in hand, we let them join our line of dabke—barefoot, stomping, heads facing the sky.

Hold On to Your Teeth

It was normally quiet in the mornings, so when wails sounded into the air like steam off of a freshly baked pie, the town was forced to awaken. More opened their eyes to their own teeth, things one rarely sees outside of a mirror. Each passing moment made it more clear that one wasn't dreaming, and as the morning grog faded from eyes, panic set in.

Clean, dry teeth sat on the townspeople's pillows. Some screamed, others sat in shock. Surely this must be an extended dream. A small mounds of teeth lay on pillows, or a patch of bedsheets, with a slight dip at the weight. Most did not scream, only gasped loudly and in such a way that for any other circumstance would have been over-dramatic, then hurried away to another household member. Maybe they would have answers. Restless sleepers scrambled to find their scattered molars while spouses worked to separate the teeth of one from the other. Most gave up on this task, dumping all teeth into some holder and rushing away. Bare feet thumped up and down wooden staircases. Away from the teeth on their pillow, to a telephone, to a mirror to examine soft gums, out the door and to a car to find someone who knew what to do.

One girl, a deep sleeper in her teens, slept through the morning frenzy entirely. She woke up later, teeth stuck to cheeks, leaving small craters and an empty house. Her family was already at the dentist's office. She gathered up her teeth and joined them.

Teeth were dry, which was quite remarkable, as they came from a mouth, a notoriously wet and sticky place. If one looked closely, they might have been able to see saliva stuck in the dark grooves of a molar in the early morning, but none did. By the time anyone examined their own teeth well, they were most certainly dry, clinking against one another like porcelain in whatever container had been close on hand that morning.

In the dentist's office, teeth were held in their hands or locked away in bags or mason jars. Waiting, patients opened and closed their mouths slowly, feeling around where teeth used to be with a tongue that had too much room. It was an unsettling feeling, like moving house, and stepping into a room one last time before leaving, but the room has been emptied of its belongings. Others snapped their mouths open and closed, as if clacking invisible teeth against one another, drawn in by the lack of a noise that followed. Some sat in corners, teeth in hand with a look that indicated hopelessness. A sort of *what am I to do without my teeth?* desperation. *Please, I'll take better care of them, give back my teeth, what am I to do without my teeth?*

Broken Villanelle for a Broken Country

When stepfather married mother's english—Cameroon divided.
Her broken   french made room for him
our home a country of two languages.

History unfolded in their union. Two halves
of Cameroon commingled. For the first time   I understood
Cameroon was a divided country   marriage couldn't

mend. My stepfather told me
Le français est la langue des voleurs   he resented
his colonial tongue   found home in our english.

When the war broke out & english Cameroon seceded
stepfather disagreed   said Cameroon was beautiful
in its forced union. Blind to the split country

fighting against itself. This war is as old as Cameroon
it's what happens when Colonial masters decide
a country's fate   leaves parents with only half languages

to give their children. I understand why stepfather never spoke
french with us   the language is beautiful but the history
gruesome. When the scramble is over   broken countries are left   to
   repair themselves
and children are left with no languages to call home.

That Boy

That boy taught us to swim.
What is he, thirteen?
The six of us are 50 or 60 years older...each.
Not every teacher has to be grown.

That boy flew in the water...on top and underneath.
We six had never even put our faces under water,
Not in a pool, not in a tub, not in a sink.
That boy amazed us.
We wanted to water-fly too.

"I feel I can fly," I told that boy.
He led us to a whole new way to travel.

Grandmother From Syria

Soft, young woman, the sun that browns your body
and dries your apricots and your laundry,
has brought you to the windowsill of a stuffy home,
and filled your ears with the downstairs neighbor's screams,
her brown face entangled in the branches
of the man she had to marry.

You sit in the sun and turn the radio louder,
even when you don't feel like music.

Soft, young woman, the sun that browns your body
keeps you at the windowsill,
the echo of each slap, each dish breaking
with the force of a falling tree, the man, the shop owner
opposing the tenacious roots of the woman, noisy neighbor,
doesn't bother you,
you've learned
you only get a good beating when you're bad.

My heart holds your stories,
I see your strong body, hear your rich, coarse voice,
bruised pomegranate, sweet and sure
like your neighbor, the sun, the music,
like your children and their children,
like me.

KATHLEEN OLESKY

The Ides of March

March. The Ides
You came to tell her
About the solitary snowdrop
That shivers in her garden.
You spoon red Jell-O onto stubborn lips.

She takes you to the brink and back
then rallies again,
a perpetual chain of final moments.

Today she sits up,
awake and smiling.
She knows she is dying
tells you not to cry because

she is not afraid
because Life is wondrous—
it's a cycle.

You say you're sorry,
she waves a bony hand
and forgives
decades of discord.

She tells you not bury the roots too deep
when you transplant her peonies and
don't turn your back on your brother.

She no longer wants to hear
about snowdrops or that
she'll see you tomorrow.
Her lips are sealed against parting
on the night table
the Jell-O has melted.

I Don't Think This Ends Well

I've seen enough to make me
think this doesn't end well.
The dark thoughts and sleepless nights
are prime to drive any sane man mad.
There's a feeling that cuts so deep,
the depth it reaches severs all that you are.
There's a truth that's so damn cold,
you forget what warmth was to begin with.
I've wandered this Earth long enough
to know there's no one waiting at the edge,
there's only you and the scars that have
followed you all the days of your life.
It's not as bad as they say,
it's not perfect, but it's you.
Although it may not end well,
it would've never been any other way.

Halphorisms

1. The poet is the boxer of the soul.

2. You can't spell o-u-b-l-i-e-t-t-e
without b-o-t-t-l-e.

3. Rockingchairs, sculpted
by the heartbeat.

4. Not stars
but bulletholes.

5. The boxer is the poet of the body.

6. Can't sing; still trust song.

7. Joy bottlenecks;
grief monsoons.

8. Tether us together
with ampersands. They'll hold.

9. All day we're assigning meaning;
all night we're awaiting confirmation's echo.

10. Not stars
but punchcards of avoidable losses.

11. All day recovering from judgment.

12. Which swing of the pendulum is this?

13. I'm trying to learn to brother this world.

14. Know pain; no pain.

Finding Uncle's Dead Body

The one who touched me
moved into 1454 before the sheriff

padlocked the door.
I'd gone to collect an apology.

I found him in the nursery
with his porn, gerbils in cages,

 and Playmates taped over
a mural of Care Bears

sharing an umbrella
under a cloud of red balloons.

His torso was twisted
across a twin mattress.

Blue of neck
alone in the cold

was not price enough.
He got off

cheap. I am still not okay

because I don't
know what to do

with myself
now that he is gone,

and I have no other target
for this hate,

but my own
incensed body.

Home Invasion

At the front door
the sticky thumb of vole scrabbling
behind the baseboard.

In the old windowpane,
blurred features of a thin shadow face
looking aside for the doorbell.

Where it had been,
two curled wires slip out of the hole,
twitching insect antennae.

Someone else's dream
trying to break into the wrong house.
Moon, a lookout hiding in the trees.

Brown Shoe

What has befallen you that led you to the center of a busy intersection, alone, at the peril of being crushed by racing cars? You remain erect and proud, as if standing at a counter of an expensive boutique, or dancing in the moonlight at a lavish cocktail party. What was your journey to this perilous intersection, brown shoe?

You resemble a fashionable, early twentieth-century, woman's ankle-high shoe with elaborate brogue design and brown silk laces. You're made of beautiful, polished, brown leather, which has aged gracefully.

Were you lovingly handmade by a master cobbler in Europe for a wealthy matron, or mass produced by immigrants for upscale shoe stores? Were you worn by a wealthy socialite or a beautiful debutante? Your size suggests you were worn by a petite woman, a blond, brunette, or redhead.

Was a man fortunate to have married your owner, or did she simply date handsome suitors for her amusement? Perhaps she was an entrepreneur, a professional woman, a corporate chieftain, or a loving homemaker.

How many exotic travels did she enjoy, and romantic encounters did she relish? What were her heartbreaks and disappointments? Did she have children? What has befallen you, beautiful brown shoe? Did you fall off the back of a thrift store truck, or did your wearer return to visit her former neighborhood of stately Victorian homes, now replaced by skyscrapers?

I pray you weren't struck in the intersection as your wearer traveled to her afternoon tea with friends, and I shudder to think you might have been worn by an elderly woman, slowly crossing the street, not making it through the crosswalk before being hit by a careless driver.

As I fight rush hour traffic to present my grandmother's eulogy, you remain in my thoughts, brown shoe. My grandmother lived to be 103 years old. She was a tireless, progressive trailblazer in business and politics. She was active in the civil rights movement, fought for equal pay and justice for women, and was an ardent environmentalist. Until the last few years of her life, she had a busy social calendar that included her beloved ballroom dance classes.

I want to rescue you, brown shoe, from being crushed in the intersection so I may cherish you as a valuable family heirloom, or give you to my daughter who might research your history.

Alas, I'm already blocks away, too late to retrieve you from the perilous intersection. I pray a kind soul will recognize your beauty, and you will find a home in an upscale vintage thrift store, clothing museum, or become a prized addition to a woman's shoe collection.

As I peer into the rear view mirror, I see an old homeless woman, pushing her shopping cart neatly packed with her life's possessions. She stops, picks you up, and gently polishes you, as if finding you in a fine boutique. She carefully places you in her shopping cart with her other prized possessions.

You reminded me of lost loves, revered, departed relatives, and inequities in our world my beloved, grandmother worked tirelessly to resolve.

My remarks at grandmother's eulogy will have new meaning. Thank you, brown shoe.

Swing Shift

I could have gone to work, driven with windows open
rain, tiny pins on my face; traffic, slow and easy
I would have missed the news: the houses falling into the hole
like old tinker toys in a child's sandbox
I could have driven all morning, tree parts sucked into my car's grille
a fallen branch here; a crushed car there

picture the tree crashing right through
the house where that family used to watch tv
now a sunken living room, furniture boats adrift

ballerina with dirty toe shoes pirouetting into the earth
the scene of the Seine, French-like and elegant
trees and stumps, broken plaster of Paris
paint mixed with mud, Moulin Rouge dripping

toys askew, broken, shattered, split
the happy clown cracks the big log legs
I used to play Cootie, putting the arms on, then the eyes,
the ears, then joyfully pulling them apart, bloodless and clean

I could have glanced casually out my windows
the winds blowing peoples' lives apart, bits of their history
riding a gust to town, the garbage cans flying by,
like little soldiers in the war-torn streets

 you would have laughed at how warm I looked
in my warm-ups drinking mocha decaf

As a Consequence of Humans

I'd schooled myself to feel no sympathy for them. I certainly felt nothing for the egg this one balanced, so carelessly, on a palm.

Well, no. I did feel something. Not for the egg, but for myself, for how hard it was to make those shell-skinned placentas that were meant to nourish a sweet, bright-eyed chick. My body had been selected over generations for this one particular flaw: it didn't produce eggs only in season. It couldn't stop making new ones, day after day, and shoving them out my cloaca.

I didn't care that humans harvested these failed births. Or I did care, because they represented our labor, and it was making humans rich. (Okay, most were only getting by—I'd seen that. But, if anything, that irked me more.) Since my escape, I'd seen humans carefully place our baby-free eggs in plastic and molded-pulp boxes. I'd seen other humans grimace as they acquired them for money.

Honestly, I didn't mind people eating our embryos. Nor did I mind foxes, nor even snakes. (Well, yes. I minded snakes.) What I hated was how humans exchanged our eggs for their strange currencies, and how overwrought it made them. In my brief study of humans, I'd followed a pack of twelve (sold for $3.99) to this house. And here I was, perched at a window, when one dropped.

"Shit!" the woman shout-whispered. "Shit shit shit!" Calcium carbonite shattered; yolk and albumin drooled onto the tile. The muscles in the woman's forehead tensed with disappointment at this lost egg, which meant lost money, which must have meant lost happiness. Thirty-three cents of lost happiness! Self-reproach spread across her face, and her eyes went shiny.

Her gaze cut toward the bedroom, where her bonded partner still slept. I'd noticed how he made her uncomfortable, how it became difficult for her to swallow when she was around him too long.

Then, unexpectedly, a smile flitted across her long, speckled face. Her body loosened as she pulled open a cupboard, took down a white bowl, and knelt, sweeping up the mess with the side of her hand. Her gaze roamed around, as if searching for someone to share this secret. (Naturally, she failed to see me.) She groaned as she rose, unsteadily, onto her feet. Now, grime and fly wings were mixed with the half-moon yolk. She whisked in milk. She put butter in a skillet. Shook in pepper. Drew in a deep, grimacing breath.

I couldn't see the man's face when she walked the plate into their bedroom, but I heard him: "Wha? I know it's not our anniversary."

...

"You know I hate breakfast."

...

"Yeah, okay, fine. Give it."

When the woman came back out, I was surprised to see her dry lips pinched. Her eyelids squeezed open and shut, as if she were sweeping back the buds of tears. I couldn't understand it, but her sadness touched mine, awakening the slumbering beast. Against my better judgment, I pecked at the window: once, twice, and three times. I thought it might distract her from the pain.

Sunset Hike After Therapy

Some branches make fists, others hold open palms.
I trace groves in bark—seek a maze outside myself.
Watch my finger like an inchworm.

Sun traces my body on a trunk—silhouette
shape held by yawning light. I retrace *the trauma*,
as evening untangles sunset—

watch as gold becomes orange becomes gray.
Day fades to stone and my mind mimics
the sky before stars and wishes.

Twilight's smudged purple forgives my knotted hair
and thought fragments. Still—your questions call
like birds on the opposite side of a lake.

I can't swim across or fly or match your pitch. I'm not sure
exactly where you are or if I could save my answers
from the stove in my chest—

before they turn to embers, fold back into the cold
crooked-current of dreams. There it seems—the hurt
is more vivid, yet less real.

Aisha

Those who knew her knew her as Shelly. I get why she changed her name, but it didn't help the way she wanted it to. Her real name was Aisha Kharobi. People didn't need to know that fact to feel uncomfortable around her. When she wore her hijab, they knew she was a Muslim. They heard her speak and knew she came from somewhere in the Middle East. They saw her skin and subconsciously associated her with terrorists. She got rid of both the veil and the name and improved her accent, but skin color is a more difficult problem to fix.

Aisha is the name of one of the prophet Muhammad's many wives. An act of charity, he asserted, since she was an orphan. She was six years old when they were married, and nine when the marriage was consummated. Muhammad had sex with a nine-year-old named Aisha.

Our Aisha's parents told her not to share her name with any Americans because they would not understand, but she was surprised when she arrived in the U.S. and found that Americans did not care what her first name was, or meant. Ancient history did not matter to them as much as recent history did.

I remember being with her at a coffee shop when this girl started talking to us. If she was at all stereotyping Aisha—Shelly—she gave no hint of it, nor of over-compensating for her ignorance. It was refreshing. Shelly was even bold enough to disagree with her at an appropriate time. The girl was saying how intolerant and corrupt American society was getting.

"Well, actually, some countries that I've heard of are much more corrupt than America. And as intolerant as Americans are, Islamic countries are more so," she shyly stated.

"How do you know?" The girl spread her arms out, gesturing around her. "Can't you see all the sexism, racism, and privilege of white people around here?"

"You don't even know sexism. Muslim women don't have any rights of their own. They can't talk or work or drive or do anything without a man giving them permission."

"Really?" Confusion hit the white girl's face.

"Yes, it's horrible over there."

"No. How can you say that about someone else's religion? This is exactly what I'm talking about, everyone is intolerant of everything now. That's their culture over there, you can't just hate them."

I expected Shelly to take off her disguise and tell her who she really was then, but she didn't. She just sat there silently. The white girl gave a victorious, I-feel-sorry-for-you smile and walked off to change the world somewhere else.

"How could you let her walk away without telling her where you're from?" I asked.

Watery tears formed in her pink eyes. "It shouldn't matter where I'm from. How don't they see how terrible Islam is?"

Inheritance

In the back of my grandmother's antique store
I overhear my grandfather chanting:
"I don't want to die. I'm afraid to die,"
and my grandmother soothes him, "I know, I know."

And she opens, opens doors, drapes, blinds and windows,
old glass lights in carillon colors,
and still he cries his fear of dying.
But I am five and the watches are asleep.

Clocks line the walls, each hushed at a separate hour.
This store is a theater of light,
crystal air, tobacco scents, and hard-bound
books clasping secret knowledge.

And now her hands guide me to the garden,
and I am all lit crystal and sun,
as the world rehearses another day.
The light stings like shattered glass,
and broken strings are blowing in the trees.

Melt

i want the colors to bleed together
to become this beautiful new
amalgamation
and become one
living breathing entity
that is full of life
bursting at the seams
of all these
greenredbluegoldblackvioletorangeyellowtealcreambrownsilver
emotions
people
lives

Gone Missing

Arrayed on the steps for one of those
elementary ceremonies, Memorial Day
or such, with a boy chosen to sing out
the anthem, Gerald, a name floats by,
a sweet voice, pure as an English choir,
who starts off a little high and when he
reaches the land of the free, those last notes
lie scattered the far side of a fence barely
out of reach, his face burning in the sun
and I have no idea what's become of him.

Mary had dropped seventh grade first try,
the baby and all, this girl so skilled with
pen and ink her drawing and an older's
judged dead equal, which the school had
never considered and offered a single prize,
so Mary allowed the other could win and
she'd get it outright come eighth, though
by then she was pregnant again, back when
you didn't always get a strike three.

Harold, he'd lay hands on your body and say
right here it could be a problem, straight
in your eye tell you *watch careful now* (which
paid off down the years), was country-raised
by folks who see the devil's work past every
shoulder, *rein this gift till you're sure who
whispers,* doing as most of us do, how we
deal with the night, parts of us like people
set on a raft, pushed out to sea.

Glimpses of Familiar Birds

They have come to the feeding box
in the birches, my mother notes
in Carr's bird guide circa 1931.
Now they do not fly away when I come.

In Kopek's orchard, abandoned 90 years,
someone has hung netted bags of suet
for black-capped chickadees *tseet, tseeting*
as they zip through the air.

The day she was dying, I sensed my mother
on a humming train waiting to leave the station
as if she were twelve again
off to summer camp.

Today in the orchard, a high-pitched fizzing in my ears
is louder than the chirps of birds or the soft sound
from nearby oaks as leaf after leaf
detach from nodes,

louder even than the dull, punctuated whistle
of a train in the valley bound for somewhere.

Bounce

Between 10% and 14% of married women will be raped at some point during their marriages.
—Statistic provided on National Coalition Against Domestic Violence website

When I said no, he
Woke me every hour.
Demanded to bounce,
Rode me like a horse.

(The way the cruel,
The ignorant ride—
Insisting, not asking.
Breaking and raging.)

It killed me, you know.
Bruised ribs, torn inside.
Also, a slow soul death.
So imagine his surprise

When this dead thing—
Mounted and stuffed—
This not-so-acquiescent prize,
Came back to life and left.

Decided to bounce.

And What Do We Know About Them?

"In this photograph, the black-dressed boy is Faerber Breiner, the youngest of three children of Fredegar Breiner, a carpenter from Lauingen who was killed in the line of duty in the Battle of Bzura. I already taught you the lesson about this battle, after which the Polish Army and the Polish state de facto ceased to exist. When you lose six-hundred-forty-six thousand soldiers, nine-hundred-and-eleven tanks, and all the airplanes you own, three hundred and twenty- six in number, it is an absolutely natural thing to quietly leave the world map. Germany had three damaged tanks and did not lose a single airplane.

"But unfortunately, four German soldiers gave their lives in this fight, the hero Fredegar Breiner, the carpenter from Lauingen, among them. Thanks to Lieutenant Hafner, his direct commander, who stood at his deathbed until the last moment, we all now know Fredegar Breiner's last words. 'Please look after my children,' he said. After that, just before dying, he also said, 'I would have liked to live through the day when I would have been accepted as a member of the National Socialist Party.'"

"Fredegar Breiner is resting now in Walhalla, together with his Iron Cross, decoration awarded post-mortem, as well as membership in the National Socialist Party. If you are a hero like Breiner the carpenter, the Party can award you this honor even after the time you could possibly devote to the Third Reich and to the German nation is over, and you are already up there, alongside Odin.

"In accordance with the information from the dossier accompanying this photograph, the second boy's name is Horstmar Falkenrath. He is the only son of Konrad Falkenrath, a distinguished professor of physics from Oberhausen who, through repeated deeds of heroism, managed to achieve the Stabsfeldwebel rank in the German Army. Professor Falkenrath is actually a member in an elite unit that is destroying its enemies somewhere on the Eastern Front.

"Would you like to know why I chose this photograph? Well, dear students, I didn't choose it. I picked it randomly from a stack of photographs of German children. And now, as a project for today's class, I will ask you to tell me why the Aryan child is unquestionably superior to children from other races.

"Correct answer, student Baumann! The determination, the daringness in these children's eyes represents the essence of this image, and this fact is more than obvious! And my second question arises by itself: Into whom do you think these children will turn in a few years, after the Party guides their aspirations?

"Correct answer, student Busch! Indeed! Siegfried and Thor! Here they are! In front of us! Immortalized for eternity! The Reich's future and the model image of any German boy! And the day when the entire world will understand the discrepancies, the differences that are clear between the Aryan race and other races is closer than you think…. And regarding the bursting entrance of Lieutenant Franke in the classroom, I thought that it is well-known that I do not like to be disturbed during lessons. Access to the classroom can be granted only with the permission…. In what way is it an emergency, Lieutenant? A mistake slipped into the dossier? In which dossier? In the dossier that came along with the photographs? You want to report that these two children are not from Germany, but from Latvia? And what do we know about them? We know nothing? So they could be two Latvian children, but just as well, they could be two Jewish children?

"Am I wrong, Lieutenant? They could be two Jewish children, couldn't they? Dear students, I declare today's lesson closed. And tomorrow, after Lieutenant Franke puts some order into these dossiers, we will pick another photograph and resume our debates about the unquestionable superiority of the Aryan race. You are dismissed."

Eulogy

After three weeks
we stepped out of our skin
and left our ruins behind.
Our misgivings have been taken
like an old dog behind the shed
and formality has expired.
It is autumn, the last of the acorns have fallen.
In the twilight grass, spiderwebs of frost
hide a thousand universes.
In the half-life of stars,
there is undiscovered light.
Some days, I think
I have forgiven you.

Hakuna Matata

my bare feet pound the earth
        my earth
my hips bounce to the beat
of steel drums
my traditional skirt
I only wear when the tourists come
skims my calves

hakuna matata, we sing
Tanzania, we sing
because
they're the only thing the white people
        understand

hakuna matata, we sing
I switch lines with the men
their faces smeared with color
in no particular pattern

my pregnant belly resists the movement
I demand from it
hakuna matata, we sing
the white people are here
Tanzania, we sing
and they won't be happy
        unless we look like they expect

Lynne's Gold

I found the gold ring in my late
sister-in-law's jewelry box
slipped it on my finger
and wore the band daily
until it broke.

Gold, I believed, remained
strong. We say *solid gold*.
But I learned from a jeweler—
gold is so soft
rings bend or break.

My sister-in-law cut down
our Christmas tree, shimmied
up oaks to shake mistletoe loose,
taught decades of middle-schoolers,
fostered one of her students.

After retirement, she led Relay
for Life teams, hauled immense
garbage bags full of pop cans
from doctors' clinics, donated
redemptions to the Cancer Society.

This week, the jeweler restored
her flattened ring to its full circle.
After a polishing, the gold glows.
If only the oncologists had found
a potion to restore her health.

Lynne, oh, Lynne,
I miss your ringing laughter,
your fourteen-karat kindness.

Red Diaper Babies

Like Ukrainian nesting dolls
we belonged to our parents   our parents to the Old Left
we were a community before communities were *in*

always a table set in winter with brisket and noodle kugel
in summer macaroni salad and lemonade
at dusk under the crape-myrtle Dotty's coffee cakes

There were horseshoes to throw   fireflies to marvel over
and always   political talk   political talk
the grownups   loud argumentative

endlessly vying for rightness
and we children   little ancillary soldiers
obedient   adoring   believing our parents were earthly Gods

who knew what was right for the world
a kind of Marxism perhaps
but they didn't tell us

about FBI visitations   deportations   the blacklist the underground
neighbors who crossed the street when they saw us coming
those who named names   their simmering fears

they didn't tell us
their secrets told us   theirs was a dangerous romance
my father's horn-rimmed glasses caught the sun's last rays

and while the grownups howled their blind passion
battered the table with their fists
insisting they were the right ones

knowing the right way to a better future
we children felt wrong!   not like others   we made plans
the crawlspace behind the attic bookcase was a good place to hide

while Stalin was murdering millions
we grew up tough   afraid
of everything and   just a little crazy

Man in Freefall Having a Word With Belief

Like Tuesday or pain—a cut is proof
of life. Charity on its back, a furious

fire. My hands have stolen flame. I keep
them close. Doubt gives shape

to sand, circles light & calls it
moon. Once, I balanced you like spinning plates. I held

the coats of killers as they stoned
your body. In trembling hands,

 I lifted you: a serpent. There,
in the reverie of doubt, I saw your face.

Pilate washed his hands with flourish, mine
have thrived in curious accommodation.

Shining artifacts of another time. See them
now in their reaching. Beyond the arms

of gravity, bodies yield, curving
toward what they know of light.

Queering Austen

I have thought of you
in lace
or faded calico

the gentle upturn
of your nose
an unassumed elegance

my cupid's bow
pressed against your marble cheek
a furtive thievery
in dormant mid-winter

let me take your handkerchief
the ribbon from your hair
let me ache a bit
at storied histories

that holy subterfuge
of the women who loved
before us

Rain on Sunday

Rain has come
lingers
too comfortable by far,
the weekend guest
no one really wanted.
Frogs hallelujah
rising creeks,
growing ponds,
drowning mice.
On this day
the sky is stooping
close to the trees
burying its runny nose
in the branches.
Rain is talking
in the quiet voice
of a Sunday morning.
Rain all day.

The Depression Pinks

The sky is baby rose again,
paint strokes too pretty

for my mood. Light squeezed
through a sieve, popping like

the top of a can. Fizzes sticky
on my hands

red
in the bottle but on skin streaking
pink

pastelled pansies
sprout up
frothy fronds

swaddled now

I wonder
when I will begin to
sprout again

All That Glistens

Camino de Santiago, Spain

I want to join the line for communion,
heartened by the compassion of this priest,
his blessing of the pilgrims
his offer of a place to sleep as albergues are full—
>   *just like an inn keeper*
>   *2000 years ago!*
His homily praises women through the ages
standing strong at the bases of their crosses—
>   *just maybe there is*
>   *a place for us!*
He invites us sojourners, as he lifts the host,
to love one another along the Way.

But my eyes slowly ascend
from the marble floor of this 600-year-old church—
>   *I'm doing the math,*
>   *flipping the history pages*
>   *watching ships come in*
up the lustrous altar that stretches to the towering ceiling.
>   *Gold, all Gold.*
Mary, Joseph, and the twelve, draped in gilt
from head to foot.
>   *I mull it over at the jewelry counter—*
but can't hear the invitation to communion any more.
>   *He's drowned out*
by the cries of the Inca, Maya, Aztec, Aymara
the beating drums of Zimbabwe, Ghana, and Mali,

then, as today,
>   *mining the heart of the sacred*
>   *and shipping it away*

Welded to my pew, I am
unable to join you.

The War

mama flosses
a photograph out of

her scrapbook's yellowed teeth;
she pulls

me into the iranian war, where
silhouettes are sticky with

mourning dew, where souls are
raked: red

autumn leaves, where
uniforms are

unfurled, hushed like lint;
i am

holding the
photograph but, my

feet have never sizzled
on bloodied turf; my tongue has never tasted

the colors of a bullet; i have never dangled
from war's web

Neighbors

a vast evergreen tree
cupressus leylandii grows
outside the music building

his strong arms sway
a solitary conductor
yet he is not lonely

through the window
stands a familiar figure
holding piano class

her arms branch the air
skilled hands placed
over her students' hands

demonstrating how to
cup the fingers gently
make a home for birds

This Morning in Elk Camp

The mountain sends the wind
down its north slope, straight into camp
A teaspoon
of wind enters the stove pipe
and bugles like a bull elk

it sets the tone for my dreams

The wind blows harder as morning approaches
ripping the roof off of the tent
revealing icy stars swimming in a navy sea sky
I stand there, holding the billowing canvas in my hands

the sails of a sinking ship

The whole mountain turns pink
A herd of elk are out on the point
The aspen stand sways—
The proud stove puffs without
a chimney

sharp, strong, alive

Roots

subterranean neural pathways
hum through a forest
sharing nutrients, signaling disease

sometimes bedded in stone,
or more often in the soil of woods,
they form a social network

intelligence and compassion
hairy ankles, fibrous branches
a dense smell of fertile womb and yeast

their unromantic gnarls
toil with grubs and worms
beneath a cairn, a lawn or bramble,

they snake through soil
and an expanse of slickrock
where a small fir tree flourishes

and I recall the image of an infant
held by a weary soldier
in a barren war zone

Safe as Houses

I fall apart left on my own,
as porch railings list, grey boards
scab over broken windows at times
easier than they can be fixed.

I marvel some make the effort,
keep themselves green
and squared
inside white pickets,

but I've let me fall to pieces,
interior walls collapse
that kept us safe
before I was tamed,

released ex-girlfriends
I hid in dreams from you,
who held my might-have-beens,
like flowers that could bloom,

freed my childhood enemies,
now dead or hobbled with age,
let them all go to sit in the ruins
holding hands with you.

Visitation

There you are again,
sitting in the blue chair at the foot of my bed.
No words.
Just there.
Always there.

You don't even startle me any more.
Your visits have become
almost normal,
though I never know when,
or what you'll be wearing.

Sometimes it's the red silk dress
you wore on your thirtieth birthday
when we each spent a week's pay
on dinner at Lutece
and celebrated with Kir Royales.

Sometimes the tweed blazer
you wore in Ireland
where we listened to the ocean
pummeling the rocks eight hundred feet
below the Cliffs of Moher.

Sometimes it's the hospital gown
you wore in the ICU,
while Micah sang Sondheim late into the night
and the nurses stopped what they were doing
for just a moment to hear a familiar refrain.

Now, when I wake
from ever more frequent dreams
in which you appear,
I have stopped asking
why you never speak,

Why you only watch from an armchair
in a corner of my mind.
No words.
Just there.
Always there.

Bonds

she stops stares at the dead pigeon
notices its mate standing by
she gently wipes aaron's dribbling mouth
wonders what gene makes the living watch over its dead
bearing witness to who aaron was is all she has left

what will i do when my reckoning day comes

she sits aaron down
puts the times on his lap
it's her memorial to his once vital life force
she reads the headlines
it seems diminishments fratricide assassinations are the only things
    fit to print
if aaron could decipher the page
change the movement would become the core of their lives
she curses the karma that turned aaron's roars into helpless yelps

what will i do when my reckoning day comes

she watches the cleaner hurriedly throw the dead bird away
as if it didn't deserve respect rituals rites
the mate ends its watch
she hopes the bird will fly into the rays of comfort and love
when death frees aaron
she'll celebrate who he was with each rising sun

what will i do when my reckoning day comes

House Bolting

The ocean has its silent caves,
Deep, quiet, and alone;
Though there be fury on the waves,
Beneath them there is none.
—Nathaniel Hawthorne, "The Ocean"

She revisits the past on a cruise around Alcatraz.
San Francisco Bay, a dozen
glass cooktops, shattered,
then restored. A pinch on the arm
becomes an experience.
I wake, longing

for a daughter who
left in September,
Katherine.

All my dreams pass like pearls,
dead fish, starved of oxygen.
I am hungry for a body that loves
more than my mother.

She lives in a desert, East of Paradise.
She lives on cheap wine & cigarettes.
Her lungs close like a vault there.
I come to bury her like a flash flood.

Off the highway, a new suburb, bone strong.
A billboard boasts of walls anchored to slab,
foundations. You can't see cancer. After she'd gone,
I spent a year unlearning childhood. In Spring, I

unchained the ocean.

Before Each Mouthful

Before each mouthful this spoon
rests beside the bowl
as the shallow turn a shovel

learns to widen, sift the dirt
for washed out roads
—it's your usual breakfast

facing the window, humming
over your shoulder
to a canvas bag growing wild

alongside the woolen socks
and rope for the hole in your chest
—you pack till there's no room

for cardboard and the dress
still wanting to go somewhere
still telling you it will be back

All I Only Ever Wanted Was My DMV License

Nothing like numbing your butt at the DMV to start wondering why anybody needs a damn license anyhow. Just to get somewhere.

I slumped myself off in a corner, lounging on one of them wavy plastic chairs, waiting to be called. Scrolling my phone for something worth passing the time. Cute little Mexican kid flops beside me, maybe Muslim, hard to tell sometimes. Girl, maybe eight or nine or so. Cute pigtails. Face not afraid of nothing.

"Whatcha playing?"

Sounded like an American. Sometimes they do.

"Nothing special."

"Can I play?"

"No. Where's your mom?"

"Busy."

"I bet."

"Where's yours?"

"You being smart?"

She gives me this slow droopy wink. "Duh!" she drawls.

I tried not to, but who couldn't help grinning at that?

"Find your momma. Don't be talking with no more strangers. Go."

Little bitty green lights at that teller looking place flash out 39. I got 38 but this colored man pops up like a track meet before I can budge.

"Dammit!"

"What?"

"You made me miss my time! That thief just stole my spot!"

"Stole it?"

"Same as!"

"What if he's Jesus?"

"He ain't Jesus!"

"Maybe not."

"You Jehovah's Witness or something?" I snapped my neck around looking for her mom. "You trying something on me?"

She shook her big eyes, and her pigtails shook too. She looked over at that thief colored man and then her eyes looked up at me. "Probably that's not Jesus," she said.

"Probably not," I said. "Jesus supposed to look all faggoty and stuff. Go find your mother."

"What if he's Jesus anyhow," she says, "and you didn't know it?"

I missed for 39. Damned if I was fixing to miss for 40, but I hadn't noticed before her elbow, bleeding. "What happened there?"

"Where?"

I tapped at my elbow so she'd look at hers. She saw the smeary blood. Just shrugged.

"Wipe your elbow."

I give her a napkin I'd saved from a cheeseburger. She wiped and looked for someplace to toss it, so I held out an open palm and she dropped it there. I tore a patch from my other napkin for her to blot on her elbow, and she did.

Then she up and says, "That's not the worst thing, if he's Jesus over there."

"What's that supposed to mean?" I says.

"What if you're Jesus and don't know it? What if God picked you and didn't tell you, and you'll never know—except if you don't do what you're supposed to do then you and everybody else goes to hell, nobody gets saved and just dies in hell forever."

"What—?!"

Where, I'm wondering, does some smartass kid come up with such bullshit except some crazy ass Jehovah's Witness mother needs to be incarcerated for abusing other people? And then Smart Aleck pretends to wrinkle up her face like this is all thunk up spontaneous.

"What—?!" I'm trying to argue again except she keeps interrupting.

"What if I'm not just some dumb kid you won't let play a phone game, but instead God's using me to speak prophecy?"

"And just what kind of nonsense prophecy?"

"41," she said.

Damned if 40 didn't flash over to 41.

"That's no prophecy!" I yelled—maybe a little louder than I meant to. People didn't look right at me, not in my eyes. Except she did. "Dammit!" I said, trying to whisper.

"You don't know," she says. "God does all kinds of crazy stuff."

"Shut your mouth!"

"All kinds."

I give her a tight-lipped look.

"Maybe my mom's finished peeing," she said. "Or maybe she's not—"

Her voice stopping all a sudden, mysterious, like she hadn't finished saying something.

"Or maybe she's not what?"

She gives me that stupid ass slow wink again, and off she trots down some hall. Smart aleck snotty little kid. Them kind of people ought to settle for stuffing flyers in mailboxes. Them kinds of things you can throw away. A minute later 42 took his time, so I saw my chance and finally squoze in.

About then Smart Aleck strolls past and waves her good arm on the way out, her mom, I guess it was, hunched over the other arm like it was broke. It's them spoiled ass smart aleck kids are the meanest, play the meanest jokes.

That license picture's not right. And I look different in the mirror. All I ever wanted was just my license.

Big Love

Talk about big love
Moving into it,
Not perfect love
Good love

Remember that spring that it
Rained for 75 days straight
Things that we thought
Were permanent floated away

Remember that spring
When my hair reverted back to
Something from childhood

You found me in the water
You found me soaking wet
You were there
With a boat, you plugged
With hope and rags
You held me as the waters continued to rise

Your kisses overshadowed their pleas for help
We two would survive together – you and I
So when you asked if we could
Go about and save others together
Help them into this patched boat
Stress the boards that promised our escape
Risk our only chance to get away

This was love, big love
If we were fortunate
And I hoped that we were
Regret would sing her sad song off-key

May I tell you about good love
Love that saves you from going under
Kisses parts of your soul while
Ever increasing the capacity of your boat.

JOHN R. WEST

A Shore of Shattered Sea Shells

Age, not time, is what we fear.
Time's like air
everywhere around us
and like air,
unless, or until, we run out of it,
pay no attention.
Age is a canyon where
rivers wear away rock:
the abrasion to every part,
large or small, of us, of everything.
This friction of living.

Contest Editor's Morning Read

A Nonet

So much depends on the mood she's in
when she first reads my manuscript
and whether her latte's hot,
and if her lover's cold,
and if she likes to
count syllables
in each line
down from
nine.

Leaving Las Cruces

Now you are gone, I make my own roadside temples.
I am like the bird that collects blue objects to
display its longing. Berries, torn bits of ribbon,
the odd pebble, common chicory flower. The candles
I light sputter out in the rain—the tide of the
ordinary always swimming away whatever it is
we think we can't live without. I practice being like a
seed, destined to split, to feel each layer peel
off and fall away. Green fuse at the center,
which performs the miracle of capturing a light
that travels 96,920,00 miles to reach us. Since
you left, I watch the flowers; sometimes I feel them
close by me, their beautiful naked faces that
neither hide nor reveal but simply are. The dew
falls silently most mornings. I sit outside on the step,
drinking coffee, and feel it appear as if by magic
on my hands, my face. Maybe we move toward each
other so desperately in order to flower; it doesn't
matter whether a relationship works or doesn't,
only that process of burning through. I know you
made me more alive, but who knew this would prove
so painful? I make temples as if I could turn us
to mere relic: silk flowers ribboned in bunches,
a few photographs, an effervescence stilled
and held. It almost works at times but who would
not be the thing itself if they could—green fuse
burning wild through every morning.

Millicent Borges Accardi, a Portuguese-American writer, is the author of four poetry books, most recently *Only More So* (Salmon Poetry). Her awards include fellowships from the National Endowment for the Arts (NEA), Fulbright, CantoMundo, Creative Capacity, the California Arts Council, The Corporation of Yaddo, Fundação Luso-Americana, and Barbara Deming Foundation. She's led poetry workshops at Keystone College, Nimrod Writers Conference, The Muse in Norfolk, Virginia, and University of Texas, Austin. Her non-fiction can be found in *The Writers Chronicle, Poets Quarterly,* and the *Portuguese American Journal.*

Charles Joseph Albert lives with his wife and three teenage boys, works as a metallurgist, and does his writing on the trolley to and fro. His work has appeared recently in *Vallum, Write City, the Amsterdam Quarterly, the Apeiron Review, the MOON, and The Literary Nest.* His first novel, *The Unsettler,* is now appearing in *SERIAL Magazine.*

Yasmeen Alkishawi is a Palestinian Venezuelan American woman. She received her bachelor's degree in creative writing from the University of South Florida. She is currently teaching English as a Peace Corps volunteer in Cambodia. Her poetry can be found in *Asterism.*

Essam M. Al-Jassim is a Saudi translator. He taught English for many years at Royal Commission schools in Jubail, Saudi Arabia. He received his bachelor's degree in foreign languages and education from King Faisal University, Hofuf. His translations appear in a variety of online and print Arabic and English literary journals. **Hamdan Atia** is an Egyptian novelist, short-story writer and critic. He was born in the Menofia Governorate in 1971. He holds a bachelor's degree in social science. His collection of short stories, *A Trader of Clouds* (2016), has achieved critical acclaim. *Temporary Life* (2020) is his latest published novel. Many of Hamdan Atia's critical studies have appeared in local and regional literary journals.

Honora Ankong is a Cameroonian-American poet. She is currently a candidate for a master's of fine arts degree in poetry at Virginia Tech. Her works explore the complexities of immigration, identity, and blackness across the diaspora.

Jodie Baeyens is a writing professor at The American Military University. She holds a master's in fine arts in creative writing with a concentration in poetry. Her poetry has most recently been featured in *Women Who Roar* and *Riza.*

Michael Ball scrambled from daily and weekly papers through business and technical pubs. Born in Oklahoma and raised in rural West Virginia, he became more citified in Manhattan and Boston. Now one of the Hyde Park Poets, he conquers his innate shyness at readings and open mics. He has moderate success placing poems in *Giffel, GOSS183 PoetsArtists, Havik 2019 Anthology, SPLASH!, It's All About Arts, Reality Break Press,* and the Robert P. Collén Competition.

Denise H. Bell defines herself as a mature, published poet. Her work delves into the lives of those living near the edge. Denise is a Brooklyn Poets Fellow; she is a proud member of Nickle Bag, a women writers collective. Her work appears in *Rattle, Tinderbox Review, Rigorous, Quail Bell, Anti Heroin Chic,* and *The Chaffeiy Review.* Denise's poem, "Remember My Name," was nominated for the Ploughshares Poem of the Year.

Sheila Black is the author of four poetry collections, most recently *Iron, Ardent* (Educe Press, 2017). She is a co-editor of *Beauty is a Verb: The New Poetry of Disability* (Cinco Puntos Press, 2011). Her poems have appeared in *Poetry, The Birmingham Review, The New York Times* and other places. She currently divides her time between San Antonio, Texas, and Washington, D.C., where she works at AWP.

Kim Brandon is an activist/poet/novelist/painter/storyteller. Kim's work was performed in three of the "50IN50" theater series. She's published in the *"Dream Catcher's Song"* anthology, *"Boundaries and Borders,"* an anthology of women of color writers (scheduled for publication), *the Hawaii Review,* and *Peregrine.* She is working on a novel and her first collection of poetry.

Joanne Fay Brown carried her passion for writing from an award-winning career in corporate communications to writing poetry and leading creative writing workshops. As an Amherst Writers & Artists instructor, she has led workshops in Oakland, Berkeley, and Oaxaca, Mexico, and currently, she leads workshops for the general community and for cancer patients and survivors in Santa Fe and Los Alamos, sponsored by the Cancer Foundation for New Mexico. Her poetry has appeared in *Persimmon Tree* and *Evening Street Review,* and she is currently working on a collection that touches on growing up in an atheist old left family in the 1950s.

Sam Burt's work may be found in journals including *Stonecoast Review, The Maine Review,* and *The Main Street Rag.* Burt lives in Iowa City where he works as a cheesemonger, eagerly awaiting graduate school admissions decisions.

Andrea K. Capere is an emerging poet and filmmaker living in Tacoma, Wash. Her poetry has been featured in the short film, "Bonfire" (2018), and has also appeared in *Dying Dahlia Review, Trillium,* and *The Matrix.* Her poetry and prose strive to be reflective, confessional, and bold.

Elinor Clark is a recent philosophy graduate hailing from Leeds in the cold and rainy north of England. She has work published in a number of journals including *Strix, Book XI, Printed Words* and *The Writing District.*

Zai Deriu attempted her first poem at six years old. She cultivated a love of reading soon after, and is now a sophomore attending an art-based high school in San Francisco specifically for creative writing. She has previously been published on The Project For Girls.

Suzanne Doerge is an emerging poet living in Ottawa, Canada, where she is facilitating AWA creative writing workshops with multicultural groups of women. She walked the Camino de Santiago, an ancient pilgrimage in Spain from which her poetry arises.

Renee Emerson was born in Tennessee and resides in Missouri. She has published poems in magazines such as *Perspectives, Still,* and *Valley Voices,* and currently teaches online courses for various universities. She is the author of *Keeping Me Still* (Winter Goose Publishing, 2014) and *Threshing Floor* (Jacar Press, 2016), and is online at www.ReneeEmerson.wordpress.com.

Walter Evans, a graduate of the University of Missouri and University of Chicago, has published a dozen short stories (*Cimarron Review, Kansas Quarterly, Chelsea,* etc.). He developed and maintains the website southernlitaudio. org. He believes the divine is omnipresent, constantly revealing itself around, beyond, and within us, and that on rare occasions, sometimes against our will, we become, as through a glass darkly, aware.

Nadia Farjami is a poet from Southern California. Her work has been recognized by *The New York Times, Cathexis Northwest Press, High Shelf Press, The Esthetic Apostle, The National Scholastic Art & Writing Awards, Prometheus Dreaming, Polyphony LIT, Youth Poet Laureate, Body Without Organs Literary Journal, Marmalade Magazine, Cagibi Literary Journal, The Athena Review,* and more.

Tova Feldmanstern lives in the San Francisco Bay area. She is a licensed clinical social worker and is currently pursuing a degree in music. Her writing has appeared in *Panoplyzine, Gravitas* and *Aurora.*

Jonathan B. Ferrini is a published author who resides in San Diego. He received his master's in fine arts degree in motion picture and television production from UCLA.

Kate Marshall Flaherty's sixth poetry book, *Radiant,* launched in 2019 with Inanna Press. She's been guiding StillPoint Writing and Editing Circles in the amazing AWA method for several years. Poetry is her lifeline.

Maya T. Garabedian is a first-generation American artist from Boise, Idaho. During her time at UC Santa Barbara, where she graduated in 2019 with a bachelor's degree in interdisciplinary studies, she worked at *The Catalyst* and *Spectrum* literary magazines. She is the recipient of the Keith Vineyard Award for Creative Writing, the Chancellor's Award for Excellence in Undergraduate Research, UCSB's CCS Most Excellent Narrative Prose Award, and the Richardson Poetry Award.

Corinna German writes with the Absaroka-Beartooth Wilderness over her shoulder. She can't live without grizzly bear tracks, wolf lichen on pines, and cow elk calling at dusk. Her work is published in anthologies and journals throughout the West.

Polly Giantonio has developed and co-facilitated workshops on creativity, poetry, and creative writing. She has mentored and facilitated discovery and learning by students of all ages. She lives in Vermont and enjoys dabbling in drawing. Her poems and interviews have appeared in various print journals and magazines, including *Poets & Writers.*

Joseph Hardy is one of a handful of writers living in Nashville, Tenn., who does
not play a musical instrument, although a friend once asked him to bring his
harmonica on a camping trip so they could throw it in the fire. His wife says
he cannot leave a room without finding out something about everyone in it,
and telling her their stories later. Joseph has a BS degree in psychology from
Stanford University. His work has been published in *Inlandia, Gyroscope, The
Tiny Journal, Sheila-Na-Gig,* and *Penultimate Peanut,* and is forthcoming
in *Seven Circle Press, The Bookends Review, Poetry City, Reality Break Press,
Glass Mountain, Funicular Magazine, Kind Writers, Pub House Books,* and
Crack the Spine Literary Magazine.

Gloria Heffernan's first full-length poetry collection, *What the Gratitude List
Said to the Bucket List,* was published in 2019 by New York Quarterly Books.
She has also written two chapbooks, *Some of Our Parts* (Finishing Line
Press), and *Hail to the Symptom* (Moonstone Press). In addition, her work
has appeared in over sixty journals including *Chautauqua Literary Journal,
Stone Canoe, Columbia Review,* and *The Healing Muse.* She holds a master's
degree from New York University and teaches at Le Moyne College and the
Downtown Writers Center in Syracuse, New York.

Hank Hobby has a comic book series titled "Ruwans," published by Keenspot
Entertainment; two children's picture books, *Where You Belong,* published
by MacLaren-Cochrane Publishing, and *Paper Wings,* published by Native
Ink Press; and an illustration called "Profit Over People," published by Raven
Chronicles.

Brandyn Johnson is an instructor of English at Black Hills State University in
western South Dakota. He holds a bachelor's degree in English and a master's
in fine arts degree in creative writing. His poetry has appeared in *Sugar
House Review, Gravel, Dunes Review,* and others. He lives in Rapid City, S.D.,
with his wife, Anna, and their daughter, Ari Lisboa.

Shawn R. Jones is the author of three books: two poetry chapbooks, *Womb Rain*
(Finishing Line Press, 2008) and *A Hole to Breathe* (Finishing Line Press,
2015). *Womb Rain* is #61 in Finishing Line Presses' New Women's Voices
Series. Her poetry has also appeared in *Essence, Challenges for the Delusional,*
and *the River Heron Review's* debut issue. Shawn is also the owner and
operator of Tailored Tutoring LLC and Kumbaya Academy, Inc. She is a
graduate of Rutgers-Camden's master's in fine arts degree program.

Gloria Keeley is a graduate of San Francisco State University with bachelor's and
master's degrees in creative writing. She collects old records and magazines.
Her work has appeared in *Spoon River Poetry Review, Chiron, Slipstream,* and
other journals.

Joshua Kepfer is a 23-year-old living in Northern California. He enjoys spending
time in the mountains and the ocean there. Much of his inspiration to write
music, prose, and poetry comes from nature and a faith in God.

Jake Kinzie is a website designer who finds writing to be the ultimate form of
self-expression. He loves writing small, tightly worded stories and essays that

echo his experiences living with OCD. He has previously been published in *Word Riot, Ascent Aspirations, Flash Fiction Magazine, Literally Stories*, and *Five on the Fifth*.

Sheree La Puma is an award-winning writer whose personal essays, fiction, and poetry have appeared in or are forthcoming in *WSQ, Juxtaprose, Heron River Review, The Rumpus, Plainsongs, The Main Street Rag, I-70 Review, The London Reader, Bordighera Press—VIA: Voices in Italian Americana*, and *PacificReview*, among others. She received a master's degree in writing from California Institute of the Arts and taught poetry to former gang members.

Sean Lause is a professor of English at Rhodes State College in Lima, Ohio. His poems have appeared in *The Minnesota Review, The Alaska Quarterly, Another Chicago Magazine, The Beloit Poetry Journal*, and *Poetry International*. His most recent book of poetry is *Midwest Theodicy* (Taj Mahal Review, 2019).

Marcia Lynx is a translator, ghost-writer, critic (*Guardian, New Republic*), and book editor who runs the ArabLit website (www.arablit.org), which won a 2017 London Book Fair prize. She also publishes *ArabLit Quarterly magazine*. Her co-translation of the middle-grade novel *Ghady and Rawan* was published last summer by University of Texas Press (August 2019), and her translation of Sonia Nimr's *Wondrous Journeys* is forthcoming (2020) from Interlink. She won the 2019 Columbia College Literary Review Editors' Prize Contest for the short story, "Tell a Stranger What You Do."

Chloe Marer is an artist overall and a writer at heart. She enjoys gardening, baking, and playing Dungeons and Dragons with her friends on the weekends. @ chloe.m.writes, Instagram.

Kathleen Olesky, who has a master's degree in fine arts, has been leading AWA workshops since 2004.

Simon Perchik is a former contributor to *Peregrine*. His poetry has also appeared in *Partisan Review, The Nation, The New Yorker*, and elsewhere.

George Perreault has worked as a visiting writer throughout the American West.

Karen Poppy's work has been published in *The American Journal of Poetry, The Gay and Lesbian Review Worldwide, ArLiJo, Wallace Stevens Journal*, and *The Cortland Review* (Best of the Net nomination). She has a chapbook forthcoming with Finishing Line Press, and another chapbook forthcoming with Homestead Lighthouse Press. She has also recently compiled her first full-length poetry collection, written her first two novels, and is at work on her second poetry collection and third novel. An attorney licensed in California and Texas, she lives in the San Francisco Bay Area.

Christine Anne Pratt has been published in *The Aurorean, The Common Ground Review*, and *Compass Roads*, an anthology of poems about the Pioneer Valley. She's spent a large part of her life working with children and literacy. Presently, she's very involved in the "Me Too" movement and understanding her own history. She lives in western Massachusetts.

Gretchen Rockwell is a queer poet and supplemental instructor of English at the Naval Academy Preparatory School in Newport, R.I. Her work has appeared in *Glass: Poets Resist, Kissing Dynamite, Noble/Gas Quarterly, FreezeRay Poetry, the Minnesota Review*, and elsewhere. Gretchen enjoys writing poetry about gender and sexuality, history, space, and unusual connections.

Lauren Rose is a junior at Sierra Nevada College double majoring in creative writing and biology, and minoring in outdoor adventure leadership. Her short story "I Belong Here" will be appearing in the 2020 Running Wild Press's *Anthology of Stories,* Vol. 4. She received the 2018 Upcoming Creative Fire award from Sierra Nevada College, and is the 2017 first-place winner and scholarship recipient for the Richard Harris Law Firm Students with a Cause Contest in the category short story, third-place winner at the 2016 Spark! Poetry Contest, and has been recognized by seven Scholastic Art and Writing Awards.

Lois Rosen's poetry books are *Pigeons* (Traprock Books, 2003) and *Nice and Loud* (Tebot Bach, 2015). She has taught English as a second language in Oregon, New York, Ecuador, Colombia, Japan, and Costa Rica. Lois co-founded the Peregrine Poets of Salem, Oregon. She leads the Institute for Continued Learning's Amherst Writing Group at Willamette University. Lois won Willamette Writers' 2016 Kay Snow Award in Fiction. Her writing has appeared in numerous publications including *New Verse News, Calyx, Willow Springs,* and *Timberline Review.*

Denzel Xavier Scott earned his bachelor's degree in English from the University of Chicago and received his master's of fine arts degree from Savannah College of Art and Design in his hometown of Savannah, Ga. His works appear in various literary magazines: *Rattle, Empty Mirror, Spillway, decomP, Euphony Journal, Blacklight Magazine, Pegasus Literary Magazine, Bombay Gin, Missing Slate, Apeiron Review, The Gambler Mag, SLAB Magazine, Linden Avenue, 3Elements Review, Cortland Review,* and t*he Louisville Review.* He is a past recipient of the University of Chicago's prestigious Summer Arts Council Fellowship Grant. In September 2018, he became one of the winners of Writer Relief's Peter K. Hixson Memorial Prize.

D.R. Shipp, originally from Texas, is an observer finding his way. A poetry finalist in the *Atlanta Review, Juxtaprose, Sycamore Review,* and *Tinderbox Journal,* his work can also be found in *Chaleur, Cleaver Magazine, Waxing & Waning,* and others. He splits his time between now and then, traveling. He has a curious online following, instagram @shippwreckage.

Travis Stephens is a tugboat captain who resides with his family in California. A graduate of University of Wisconsin-Eau Claire, recent credits include: *Gyroscope Review, 2river, Gravitas, Sheila-Na-Gig, Raw Art Review, Crosswinds Poetry Journal, Sky Island Journal,* and *The Dead Mule School of Southern Literature.*

Ron Stottlemyer lives in Helena, Mt. After a long career of teaching and scholarship at colleges and universities—Tusculum College, The University of

Tennessee, The University of Arizona, and Carroll College—he is returning to his love of writing poetry. His work has appeared in *Alabama Literary Review*, *The Sow's Ear*, *The American Journal of Poetry*, *Streetlight Magazine*, *Stirring*, *West Texas Literary Review*, *Temenos*, *South Florida Poetry Journal*, *Twyckenham Notes*, *Split Rock Review*, *Rust and Moth*, *The Worcester Review*, and *The MockingHeart Review*. One of his poems, "Falling," (*Twyckenham Notes*, Summer 2018) has won a Pushcart Prize and will appear in the 2020 edition of the prize works.

Alison Terjek is a poet and avid hiker living in northwest Connecticut. She spends her weekends exploring trails throughout New England where she finds inspiration and healing in the mountains. From 2017 to 2019 she was a Service to Improve Community Health AmeriCorps member. Her work has been published in *Causeway Lit*, *Northern New England Review*, *The Adirondack Review*, and *Burningword Literary Journal*.

Brett Thompson has been writing poetry since his graduate days at the University of New Hampshire where he earned a master's degree in English writing with a concentration in poetry. He has been published in various journals, including *Tilde*, *The Charles Carter*, *District Lit*, *The Literary Nest*, *Cobalt Review*, and *Ink in Thirds*. He teaches and lives in New Hampshire with his wife and two young daughters, who both love owls and anything purple.

Răzvan Ursuleanu is a radio show host for Romanian Radio. He wrote, under the pen name Alexander MacLennan, the book *Letters and Pictures from the Great War*, which inspired a radio theatre series with the same title. He is an actor, too, and performed the leading role in "Explosive" by Elise Wilk. This radio theatre drama won Asia-Pacific Broadcasting Union's contest in 2017, Gran Prix Marulic in 2018, and New York Festivals in 2018. He is also the co-director of the short radio theater drama "Heruvim," winner of the silver medal at UK Radio Drama Festival 2019. Another theatrical piece written by him, "Come Back to Me, Marge Piercy," was selected for the 2019 edition of the GI60 Festival—The Home of Tiny Theater, and was presented to the public at Stage@Leeds Theatre.

John R. West is a retired librarian, classified as white, though realizes such classification is meaningless except to census takers and assholes, though it has not been lost on him, ever, the privilege that has meant. He is 68, which means what? He lives in north Texas with his wife, three dogs, and two cats. He doesn't give a rat's patoot who marries who, loves who, or is whomever, as these are matters of the heart and that metaphor is such a mystery. A citizen of Canada, he has lived in the United States since he was 13. You can do the math. He thinks Dr. Fiona Hill expressed why people come to the U.S. hoping for a better life, or at the least, a chance at a better life.

Susan Whelehan recently had her first collection of poetry published by Piquant Press, *The Sky Laughs at Borders*. Her face still hurts from smiling. She writes, makes art, sings, supports refugees, and leads AWA gatherings in her home in Toronto that she shares with her husband. Her sons could call more often. She hopes they have read her book.

Nicole Zelniker is an editor at *The Conversation US* and a podcast producer at "The Nasiona." She has published several pieces of poetry and short stories as well as *Mixed,* a non-fiction book about race and mixed-race families, and *Last Dance,* a collection of short stories. Read more of her work at nicolezelniker.com.

Peregrine

The Journal of Amherst Writers & Artists

Peregrine has provided a forum for national and international writers since 1983, and is committed to finding exceptional work by both emerging and established writers. We seek work that is unpretentious, memorable, and reflects diversity of voice. We accept only original and unpublished poetry and short stories. No work for or by children. *Peregrine*, published by Amherst Writers & Artists Press, is staffed by volunteers. All decisions are made by the editors after all submissions have arrived, so our response time may be slower than that of other literary journals. We welcome simultaneous submissions.

Poetry: Three single-spaced, one-page poems. We seek poems that inform and surprise us.

Prose: Short stories, double-spaced, 750 words maximum (include word count on first page); shorter stories have a better chance.

For additional submission details, please see www.amherstwriters. com or peregrinejournal.submittable.com. All submissions are via submittable.com unless other arrangements are made.

Additional copies of this issue are available at amazon.com for $12.

The Editors

Amherst Writers & Artists Press
P.O. Box 1076
Amherst, MA 01004
www.amherstwriters.org